T0095512

THE MALI EMPIRE

THE COMPLETE HISTORY OF THE MALI EMPIRE

J.P.MARTIN

ISBN: 978-1-6987-1358-8 (sc)
ISBN: 978-1-6987-1357-1 (e)

The quotes mentioned are from Ibn Battuta Travels In Asia And Africa 1325-1354 Published under the Authority of the Maharaja Sayajirao University of Baroda, Baroda

Trafford rev. 01/18/2023

 www.trafford.com

North America & international
toll-free: 844-688-6899 (USA & Canada)
fax: 812 355 4082

CONTENTS

ACKNOWLEDGEMENTS

This book is dedicated to my creator to whom I am eternally grateful. This book is also dedicated to all of my family.

By J.P. Martin

INTRODUCTION

The Mali Empire was one of the most prosperous and powerful empires in the antiquity of Africa. Its growth and expansion from the thirteenth century onward was legendary and pivotal in the history and indeed the culture of western Africa. From their control over the Trans-Saharan trade routes to their influential royal class who produced notable kings such as Mansa Musa, the Mali Empire made a significant impression. This book conveys the full historical record of this great nation and delves into the rich culture, religion, architecture, societal organization, royalty, and commercial activities of this great empire. The epic landmark events of the Mali Empire are captured and clearly explained in detail within this text and come complete with images and illustrations. The comprehensive historical record of the Mali Empire is kept alive for all to enjoy, remember, and revere within this book. The account of the Mali Empire showcases some of the best African achievements and African history.

West African Gold Nuggets

CHAPTER 1

An Introduction to West Africa

Map of Africa in the Present Day

Africa is the second-largest continent on earth, with a total land area of 11,724,000 square miles. The continent also includes a number of surrounding islands and comprises a total of 20 percent of earth's land area. Africa is surrounded by six continents: Europe to the north, North America and South America to the west, Asia and Australasia to the east, and Antarctica to the south. Africa is also the birthplace of the first human beings on earth, and these Africans created the first human civilizations. Africans were first established on earth in around 260,000 BC and eventually went on to colonize the entire planet. From around 80,000 BC, Africans began to expand into other regions of the planet. West Africa is a vast region with a mostly hot climate and rich ecology. Located to the west of the region is the Atlantic Ocean. The majority of West Africa is flat, although the region stands well above sea level.

At the present time, modern-day western Africa consists of a number of countries, including Benin, Burkina Faso, Cameroon, Chad, Ivory Coast, Gambia, Ghana, Guinea, Guinea-Bissau, Liberia, Mali, Mauritania, Niger, Nigeria, Senegal, Sierra Leone, Togo, and the island nation of Cape Verde. West Africa is also home to hundreds of different languages and ethnic groups. Rock engravings and cave paintings that date back to 7000 BC in the area of modern-day northern Chad, specifically in the Tibesti mountain area, depict early Africans hunting and herding animals. Around two hundred engraving sites and one hundred painting sites have been identified within the region, and many portray warriors dressed and armed with spears, bows, knives, and shields. The Sahara region stretches from western Africa to eastern Africa and also encompasses much of northern Africa. The Sahara region prior to 5000 BC included a large number of rivers and lakes, but by 3000 BC, the area began to dry out. The southern fringe of the Sahara is called the Sahel. West Africans operated throughout both the western Sahara and the Sahel.

Within the Sahel, there was enough grass for goats, sheep, and cattle to graze. It is thought that farming in West Africa was invented independently from other parts of the planet. The soil was fertile enough for West African farmers to grow grains such as sorghum, millet, and fonio. Millet and sorghum were used in the preparation of cakes, flatbreads, and porridge. The West Africans also farmed African rice and grew vegetables such as okra and yams. African rice was developed from a wild grass that grew within water holes, and in addition, they were able to cultivate oil palm from palm trees. The West Africans also began working with iron in around 2500 BC, and this was the beginning of West Africa's Iron Age. Evidence of working with iron

2

and iron smelting has been found in the region of Lejja in Southeastern Nigeria just prior to 2000 BC. Smelting is the process of extracting base metals from ores by heating them. Slag is a by-product of smelting ores. Within the main village square in Lejja, remains of over eight hundred slag blocks weighing between thirty-four and fifty-seven kilograms have been found. The West Africans also heavily leveraged the Niger River. With a length of 2,600 miles, the Niger River is the third-longest river in Africa after the Nile River and the Congo River. The Niger River cuts through the modern-day countries of Guinea, Benin, Niger, Mali, and Nigeria and eventually empties into the Atlantic Ocean.

The Niger River supported surrounding populations of fishermen, herders, and farmers. Local fishermen used nets and spears to capture the varieties of life which lived in the water. The river was used as a means of transportation of both people and goods across western Africa and supported trade. Western Africa also had the largest concentration of ancient kingdoms and empires on the continent. Some of the more well-known kingdoms and empires include the Nok Kingdom which was established in 1000 BC. Other civilizations include the Ghana Empire, the Songhai Empire, the Sokoto Caliphate, the Kanem Empire, the Oyo Empire, the Wolof Empire, the Ashanti Empire, the Kingdom of Ife, the Kingdom of Dahomey, the Benin Empire, the Mossi Kingdoms, the Kingdom of Takrur, and the Hausa Kingdoms. The Hausa Kingdoms included seven states namely Daura, Kano, Katsina, Gobir, Rano, Biram, and Zazzau, located in the region of modern-day northern Nigeria. The Mali Empire would become one of the largest and most powerful of the West African empires. The three great western African powers in terms of sheer scale and influence were the Ghana Empire, the Songhai Empire, and the Mali Empire.

The Mande people are a group of West Africans who all speak the Mande languages. The Mande people are further subdivided into smaller ethnic groups. The largest of the Mande groups is the Mandinka (also known as the Malinke). Other large Mande groups include the Bambara, Dyula, Soninke, Susu, Ligbi, Vai, and the Bissa. The Ghana Empire, which was the first of the great powers, was established in AD 300 and was founded by the Soninke people. Subgroups of the Soninke include the Wangara and Maraka. The first ruler of the Ghana Empire was said to be a ruler named King Dinga Cisse. The Ghana Empire was also known as the Empire of Wagadou. The empire covered a much larger region than modern-day Ghana; the total region encapsulated modern-day Mali, southern Mauritania, eastern Senegal, and Gambia. King Dinga Cisse established the city of Koumbi Saleh as the capital of the empire. The Ghana Empire eventually went on to develop an army of two hundred thousand, of whom forty thousand were skilled archers.

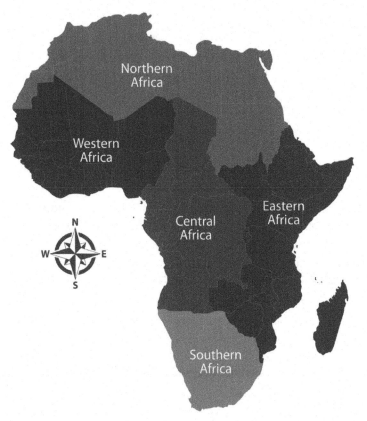

Map of Africa

The Ghana Empire also eventually controlled a large portion of both the gold and salt trade in the region and a significant portion of the Trans-Saharan trade routes. The empire also became prosperous because of its location, which was between the Senegal River and the Niger River.

The trade routes that the Ghana Empire controlled included the transport and trade of goods such as luxury garments, knives, copperware, glass, silk, velvet, brocade, glass, porcelain beads, jewelry, salt, mirrors, kola nuts, carpets, perfumes, copper, horses, paper, tea, coffee, ivory, gum, ostrich feathers, animal hides, ink, textiles, sugar, and most importantly, gold.

Indeed, the empire became wealthy because of the salt and gold trade between West Africans and the Berbers of North Africa. The Berbers are an African ethnic group that has inhabited North Africa since 10,000 BC and are indigenous to the north African region—sometimes called the Maghreb. The Maghreb includes the countries of modern-day eastern Mauritania, western Sahara, Morocco, Algeria, Tunisia, Libya, northern Mali, and northern Niger. The Berbers used camels to carry salt from North Africa to the Ghana Empire and trade it for gold. One of the reasons such commercial development was made possible was the introduction of the camel into North Africa. The camel has been referred to as the 'ship of the desert' because of its unique physical characteristics which allow the camel to survive in extremely dry climates and carry large loads of goods for many days with limited water and food.

Within the Ghana Empire, donkeys were used to transport goods. The Ghana Empire's location enabled the Soninke people to completely control commerce from the forest zones in the south, the Sahara region, and the Maghreb in northwestern Africa. In addition to gold, cowrie shells were also used as currency within the West African markets. Approximately 125 miles north of the city of Koumbi Saleh was the city of Audoghast (also translated as Awadaghust). It was located in the region of modern-day Mauritania. It came under the control of the Ghana Empire and operated as another important commercial city. Again, trade between the West African Soninke and the North African Berbers continued. The most powerful Berber clans at this time were the Tuareg, Mauri, Masmuda, Zenata, and the Sanhaja, many of which adopted the religion of Islam. At this time, a small portion of the Africans within the Ghana Empire was Muslim, but most retained traditional African belief systems. For example, the city of Koumbi Saleh became a center for Islamic learning but was split into two sections, an Islamic sector and a non-Islamic sector. Indeed, the city of Audoghast sat on a trade route for gold that was shipped northward to the city of Sijilmasa in southern Morocco where gold was then minted. Typically, the journey from Audoghast to Sijilmasa took approximately two months.

Eventually, some of the major Berber tribes combined their forces to create an Islamic African group known as the Almoravids which quickly grew in strength and influence by implementing adherence to strict Islamic law. Over time, the influence of the Ghana Empire began to decline. For example, by AD 1056, the Almoravids were successful in taking control of the city of Audoghast. The African Berber territory at this time covered the region of modern-day Morocco, western Sahara, Algeria, northern Libya, and Mauretania. The term "Almoravid" translates as "one who is ready for battle at a fortress." There were a number of other reasons for the Ghana Empires' decline. Firstly, the kings of Ghana slowly began to lose their trading monopoly. At the same time, drought was beginning to have a long-term effect on the land and its ability to sustain cattle and cultivation. In the eleventh and twelfth centuries, new gold fields began to be mined at Bure (located in modern-day Guinea) out of the commercial reach of Ghana, and new trade routes were opening up farther east. Because of the growing influence of Islam in western Africa at this time, the majority of the region formerly surrounding the Ghana Empire eventually became Islamic. A further contributor to the decline of the Ghana Empire was the rise of the African military leader called Sumanguru who was from the Susu tribe. The Susu people are a Mande ethnic group living primarily in the modern-day countries of Guinea and northwestern Sierra Leone. He launched a series of military campaigns against the waning power of the Ghana Empire. His rule eventually led to a military conflict. Finally, the Ghana Empire would split into twelve separate smaller kingdoms, each ruled by a separate prince. By AD 1200, the dominance of the Ghana Empire in western Africa came to an end.

CHAPTER 2

Early Mali

Mali, West Africa, Djenne (Mosque)

The decline of the Ghana Empire left a power vacuum of sorts within western Africa. Just south of the Ghana Empire, the Kingdom of Kangaba had been established by the Mandinka ethnic group prior to the decline of the Ghana Empire in AD 750. The Mandinka people were a subgroup of the Mandé people and were also known as the Malinke and the Maninka. A number of Mandinka chiefdoms had been established around the area of the upper Niger River, with Kangaba being the most prominent. New sources of gold were located and mined at Bure, which was south of the city of Koumbi Saleh, and attracted the Mandinka. Previously, the Kingdom of Kangaba had fallen under the control of the Ghana Empire after its expansion across western Africa. Once the Ghana Empire declined and was broken up into twelve separate kingdoms, Kangaba was again able to rise as an independent nation. Just prior to the official founding of the Mali Empire, there were numerous kings and queens of Mali, and this period of time is sometimes referred to as pre-imperial Mali. The Mandinka also produced the Keita clan (also known as the Keita Dynasty), which was a ruling class of West African Muslims and had a large amount of political power in the region. One of the early rulers among the Mandinka was King Barmandana, who came to power in AD 1050. King Barmandana had converted to Islam as was the custom for much of the leadership in the region at this time. King Barmandana made a pilgrimage to the holy city of Mecca in Arabia (in modern-day Saudi Arabia) as was customary.

The Susu tribe (also known as the Soso) was another subgroup of the Mande people located within the region and had established a kingdom that grew in influence after the decline of the Ghana Empire. The Susu was ruled by a powerful family of blacksmiths with the family name of Kante. Blacksmiths were masters of working with iron ore and held a high position as their knowledge enabled them to use fire to turn raw iron ore into weapons and tools, which were essential for the kingdom. The leader of the Susu at the time was Sumanguru (also known as Sumanguru Kante), who had engaged in military conflict with the Ghana Empire and achieved some successes.

Mosque in Bandiagara (Mali)

After conquering many small states to the north and west (most of the former tributaries of the Ghana Empire), the Susu was soon able to take over the city of Koumbi Saleh. Sumanguru had a reputation as a cruel and ruthless warrior who was keen to adhere to the traditional religion of the Susu and practice magic, which probably contributed to the disaffection of the predominantly Muslim merchant class. Sumanguru also established a very high taxation policy and also had a reputation for mistreating Mandinka women. He was successful in conquering some local Mandinka chiefdoms and adding them to the Susu's sphere of control. The Susu soon began to launch attacks against the Kingdom of Kangaba.

CHAPTER 3

King Sundiata Keita

The Great Mosque of Djenné, Mali

Sundiata Keita was a prince from the Mandinka Keita Dynasty, which developed as the ruling class of the Kingdom of Kangaba. The oral traditions relating to Sundiata Keita were passed down generation after generation by the local griots. The griots were West African historians, storytellers, poets, singers, and musicians. Sundiata Keita's name means "lion prince" or "hungering lion." He was a warrior-king who united a scattered people, and under his benevolent leadership, he ushered in a glorious period of peace and prosperity in the region. According to the oral tradition of Mali, the wise men and diviners of the kingdom had predicted the birth of a great leader and warrior who would be the son of the current ruler named Maghan Konfara. Maghan Konfara at the time had multiple wives; however, he would soon marry a new wife named Sogolon Conde. Sogolon Conde was known as a wise woman and also a sorceress, and she fell pregnant and eventually gave birth to Sundiata Keita in around AD 1210. Maghan Konfara provided Sundiata with his own personal griot named Balla Fasseke, who would provide the young prince with wisdom and guidance. One of Maghan Konfara's other wives had a son who was born before Sundiata. The other wife was well aware that the diviners had predicted the birth of a great leader but was determined that her own son should eventually be the ruler of the kingdom. As a consequence, Sogolon Conde was concerned for the safety of her son and her other children. Growing up, Sundiata became well-known as a skillful warrior, hunter, and military strategist. According to the oral tradition of Mali, when Sundiata Keita's father died, he was exiled by his half-brother, and he had to leave the kingdom. Sundiata vowed to return and reclaim the throne of his people someday.

After this incident, Sundiata and his mother settled in a neighboring kingdom. Meanwhile, the Susu under the leadership of Sumanguru Kante continued to attack the Kangaba and the neighboring regions, killing leaders and taking tribute from them, and imposed restrictions on trade in parts of their territory. Eventually, the Mandinka people started to revolt against Sumangara, and fearing retaliation, the then ruler of the Kingdom of Kangaba fled the kingdom. Nana Triban, who was Sundiata's sister, had been forced to marry Sumanguru after some of his conquests but was secretly working against him and communicating with her brother. The people of the Mandinka requested Sundiata to return and liberate his homeland. Sundiata Keita quickly returned from exile to the Kangaba region and became the leader of the Mandinka tribe, and after meeting with allies and friends, he gathered an army and engaged in a war with Sumanguru. Sundiata Keita faced off against Sumanguru at the Battle of Kirina. The Battle of Kirina is also known as the Siege of Kirina. The details regarding both the story of Sundiata Keita and the Battle of Kirina are detailed within the *Epic of Sundiata*.

The Epic of Sundiata

The Epic of Sundiata is a classic African legend in the form of a poem that details the rise of King Sundiata and the creation of the Mali Empire. There is no single or authoritative version. To communicate much of their history the people of West Africa established an oral tradition, as well as written history, whereby information, knowledge, customs, and stories were passed down through the generations orally by griots who were west African historians and storytellers. The griots were known to have extraordinary memories and also used poetry and songs to transfer the information they had to their communities. The *Epic of Sundiata* contains many episodes and covers the entire story concerning Sundiata Keita, including the early history of pre-imperial Mali, the lineage of Sundiata, the birth and childhood of Sundiata, the surrounding African kingdoms and tribes such as the Susu, the war between Sundiata Keita and Sumanguru (which is also known as the Battle of Kirina), his exile, his eventual return and war with Sumanguru, and also the creation of the Mali Empire. The *Epic of Sundiata*, once only in oral form, was eventually written down.

The Battle of Kirina

Once King Sundiata Keita decided to facilitate the request of the Mandinka people, he was able to start organizing his own army, as well as the troops from small neighboring nations. King Sundiata Keita had the intention of engaging in direct military conflict with the oppressive Susu regime. This event in West African history culminated in the great Battle of Kirina. To put it simply, the Battle of Kirina was a war that took place between the military forces of King Sundiata, his Mandinka troops, and their allies and the military forces of King Sumanguru and the Susu. From neighboring kingdoms, King Sundiata Keita was able to create a force with a large amount of cavalry and equip them with war drums, lances, and swords. Using his strong leadership and negotiation skills, he was able to slowly gather the support of various Mandinka clans. King Sundiata was also able to gain support from the region of Tabon, directly from the King of Tabon and his son who was named Fran Kamara.

Sundiata traveled with his troops and arrived at the mountains overlooking Tabon; he saw the area full of the Susu army. Some of Sundiata's generals were concerned, requesting that any initial battle be delayed to the next day because of some fatigue the soldiers had. However, the king was keen to press forward and engage the enemy.

He led the army into battle to encourage them. This initial conflict took place near Tabon between King Sundiata Keita and some of the forces of the Susu who were taken by surprise. Concerning the details of the battle, the West African griots mention the following:

"Sundiata was in the midst of the Susu like a lion among its prey."

The Susu troops were quickly defeated. The army of Sundiata celebrated their first victory, and news of the battle and its outcome soon spread across the region, reaching King Sumanguru and the neighboring kingdoms. After this initial victory, King Sundiata continued to press forward, eventually engaging King Sumanguru and his army in a valley. The Mandinka soldiers used war drums and trumpets to intimidate the enemy as was the custom during a battle at that time. This time, Sumanguru himself was present at the battle and led his army. Sundiata organized his army into a square formation, with cavalry leading from the front and his archers at the rear. Sumanguru's soldiers ran down into the valley, attempting to encircle Sundiata and his men. However, Sundiata's army was quickly able to maneuver and reposition the archers to launch a volley of arrows at the Susu army.

The Susu began to retreat, and Sumanguru decided to end the engagement. The next day, King Sundiata would again engage Sumanguru in battle early in the morning in the region called Koulikoro. Koulikoro is located in modern-day southwestern Mali. Yet again, Sumanguru marched out to meet Sundiata. This final engagement was known as the Battle of Kirina and took place in AD 1235. The drums sounded and the battle began. Sundiata and his army charged at the Susu with their soldiers on horseback as his archers shot a barrage of arrows. After much fighting back and forth between the two forces, an opportunity was seized by King Sundiata, which would deliver a psychological blow to his enemy. Sundiata drew back an arrow and aimed it directly at Sumanguru before releasing it. He hit the Susu king, and the now-wounded Sumanguru began to retreat. The forces of Sumangaru saw their king leave, and they in turned and fled. It was a complete victory for Sundiata.

CHAPTER 4

The Establishment of the Mali Empire

Timbuktu and the University of Sankoré, Mali Empire

Subsequent to the victory at the Battle of Kirina in AD 1235, King Sundiata began the unification of Mali. It was at this time that what is known as imperial Mali was created, and the capital of this new empire was moved to Niani, which is in the Kankan region of modern-day Guinea. Niani was located to the north of the Sankarani River and east of the Niger River. Niani was also located near the lucrative Bambuk and Bure goldfields. Niani would remain the capital of the Mali Empire for more than 300 years. We find one of the best descriptions of Niani during Sundiata's reign in the form of a praise song written by the griots of the Mali Empire at the time:

"If you want salt . . . if you want gold . . . if you want cloth, go to Niani, for the Mecca road passes by Niani. If you want fish, go to Niani, for it is there that the fishermen of Moauti and Djenne come to sell their catches. If you want meat, go to Niani, the country of the great hunters and the land of the ox and the sheep.

If you want to see an army, go to Niani, for it is there that the united forces of Mali are found. If you want to see a great king, go to Niani, for it is there that the son of Sogolon lives, the man with two names."

Ibn Battuta was a North African Berber Muslim historian born in AD 1304 who traveled around north and western Africa and visited the Mali Empire. Ibn Battuta, in addition to Africa, traveled to the middle-east and Asia, including China. He provides the following account concerning the city of Niani:

"My stay at Niani lasted about fifty days, and I was shown honor and entertained by its inhabitants . . . They are seldom unjust and have a greater abhorrence of injustice than any other people. Their sultan shows no mercy to anyone who is guilty of the least act of it. There is complete security in their country. Neither traveler nor inhabitant in it has anything to fear from robbers or men of violence."

King Sundiata Keita became a Muslim and followed the religion of Islam as was the custom with the elite class in western Africa at the time; however, he also maintained the traditions, customs, and some spiritual practices. The religion of Islam is one of the three Abrahamic religions, the other two being Judaism and Christianity. The term Islam means "submission" or more specifically, "total submission to the will of God." Islam was brought to Arabia by the Prophet Muhammed, although it is understood within the religion that Prophet Muhammed taught exactly the same message as all the prophets in the Abrahamic religions including but not limited to Adam, Noah, Moses, Abraham, David, Solomon, and Jesus. Prophet Muhammed is considered to be the final prophet of God or the "seal of the prophets."

It is worth noting a mixture of Islamic customs and traditional West African customs became commonplace. From this time onward, it was also decreed that all future kings would be selected from the Keita clan. One of the benefits of the victory of King Sundiata over the Susu and Sumanguru was numerous West African territories fell either under his control or were allied to him. These lands were known as the Twelve Doors of Mali. The lands included the following: Zaghari, Tabon, Kir, Oualata, Siby, Toron, Do, Djedeba, Bambougou, Jalo, Kaniaga, and the lands of the Bozo people, who were located along the Niger River.

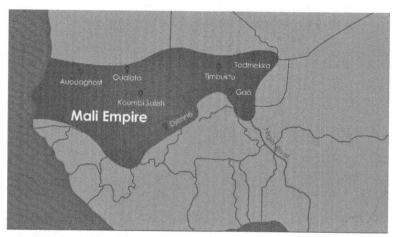

Map of the Mali Empire

In addition to his military prowess and bravery, he is revered in the history of West Africa as a great king known for his kindness, wit, and a good sense of humor; he was often asked to resolve disputes among other rulers. In AD 1240, King Sundiata seized the city of Koumbi Saleh (also known as Kumbi), essentially putting an end to the dominance of the Ghana Empire in western Africa. Koumbi Saleh had been the capital city of the Ghana Empire previously. The Mali Empire was already prospering because of its agricultural exploits, but by seizing what remained of the Ghana Empire, Sundiata also gained their salt and gold resources, which further drove the newly formed empire's prosperity. The second ruler and son of the Sundiata was Uli I (also known as Mansa Wali), and he took on the title of Mansa.

Mansa is a Mandinka word that means "king" or "emperor," and the title was taken by the royal line of Malian rulers from this time onward. He was also known as Gbèrè, which is a Mandinka word that means "red" in reference to his reddish-brown skin tone. Mansa Uli I was a devout Muslim and also made his pilgrimage to the holy city of Mecca in Arabia (modern-day Saudi Arabia). Mansa Uli I continued the expansion of the empire with the conquest of Bambuk near the Faleme River (modern-day western Mali) and also Bundu near the upper course of the Gambia River (modern-day eastern Senegal).

Mosque in Mopti, Mali

The territory of the Mali Empire expanded further, and the Mali Empire increased the revenue and wealth of the empire by opening the copper mines of Takedda (modern-day Azelik) in the east of the kingdom. Mansa Uli I was instrumental in the increased focus on agriculture for the empire. Now that relative peace had been established in the land, he implemented a large retraining program that encouraged former soldiers to become farmers and produce crops to feed the population.

They grew grains, beans, rice, sorghum, millet, papaya, gourds, calabashes, cotton, and peanuts. In addition, they raised poultry, cattle, sheep, and goats. Harvests took place in November and December just prior to the rainy season, and any surplus of food could then be sold. As such, Mali became relatively successful and prosperous within the arena of farming. The empire was divided geographically into different provinces, and the Mansa (king) delegated power to governors who oversaw each province. The courts of the empire were divided into Islamic courts and also non-Islamic courts for the inhabitants of the empire. Within the Mali Empire, a class of officials to govern specific industries was established, and these were made up of people from important families. They were known as noblemen, and they were also called ferbers.

These noblemen would have titles such as the minister of finance, minister of agriculture, and minister of fishing. The structure of the empire required a complex network of rulers and ministers because of its scale. The ferbers were picked directly by the current ruler to ensure they could be trusted and replaced should they need to be. The ferbers also had the ability to raise a small army to defend against any attacks from hostile groups, both internally and externally. The post of a ferber was extremely prestigious and important and could also be inherited by family members with the permission of the current ruler. Each important town had inspectors called mochrifs, and royal tax collectors were stationed at every marketplace. The empire collected taxes on everything that was traded. If something was traded in the Mali Empire, it was taxed. If a merchant had to travel through the Mali Empire to trade something, he was taxed. If the Mali Empire traded something with another kingdom, state, or country, it was taxed. Furthermore, there were many rules on trade; for example, all gold, which was often used almost like currency (until the introduction of cowrie shells), belonged entirely to the king. That being said, gold dust could legally be traded.

Law and order prevailed, so merchants and their caravans were able to travel easily across the empire. Within the empire, the Mandinka were grouped into different clans, with the Keita clan being the ruling clan from which the majority of the kings came. Within each clan, there were groups or castes which were focused on specific functions such as merchants, Islamic scholars, artisans, soldiers, farmers, griots, fishermen, and hunters. As was the custom among the Mandinka, when males reached the age of twelve, they would enter a caste and learn the requisite skills needed to perform a specific set of roles. When females were of age, they typically married and were responsible for teaching and raising children and looking after their households. In AD 1285, a ruler named Mansa Sakura came to power to rule the empire. One interesting fact concerning his rise to power was that he was the only king in the empire's long history that did not come from a royal bloodline. Under the leadership of Mansa Sakura, the Mali Empire was able to further expand the territory under its control by making a number of new conquests. He extended the empire along the Gambia River toward the Atlantic Ocean to the west and also the territory to the east. Mansa Sakura also encouraged trading activities, and an increased number of Berber merchants from northern Africa began traveling to Mali to engage in commerce.

CHAPTER 5

Mansa Abubakari II

The Atlantic Ocean

The Mali Empire continued to thrive and was led by a series of kings after Mansa Sakura, and rulers were again selected from the Keita Dynasty as they had been before. The ninth emperor of the Mali Empire was called Mansa Abubakri II, and he came to power in AD 1310. Mansa Abubakri II imposed a nonmilitant style of rule over the empire. Mansa Abubakri II was known to be an avid traveler and a devout Muslim and had an insatiable desire for knowledge. Having traveled all across western Africa, he was interested in discovering new lands for the Mali Empire, and specifically, he was interested in traveling across the Atlantic Ocean, which lay to the west of the empire. With this ambition in mind, he commanded the men of the empire to construct a series of large fleets of boats suitable for a long-distance voyage. He leveraged the knowledge and expertise of the shipbuilders of the empire.

He also created crews of sailors, merchants, scholars, builders, artists, and soldiers with the interest of traveling west in the direction of the Americas. With the ships constructed, Mansa Abubakri II arranged for a fleet to be sent out while he remained in West Africa. In total, a fleet of two hundred boats set sail across the ocean for the new lands. After a time, one boat of Malians returned on its own, and the crew informed Mansa Abubakri II that they had lost contact with the rest of the fleet.

Mansa Abubakri II was keen to become more involved with the operation and join the exploration himself. With this in mind, he decided to abdicate his throne so that he could lead a second and larger fleet of ships directly and join the voyage. Mansa Abubakri II placed another king in charge of ruling the Mali Empire, and this king was known as Mansa Musa. For the second voyage, the king had two thousand ships constructed. The ships were loaded with enough supplies for two years and included food, drink, medicine, and gold, which was abundant in the Mali Empire. The king again had crews composed of not just sailors and navigators but also traders, warriors, doctors, and mystics. Mansa Abubakri II traveled west along the Senegal River to the coast of the Atlantic Ocean and set sail with his huge new fleet in AD 1311.

After Mansa Abubakri II had set sail, the new king Mansa Musa became the ruler of Mali and eventually the wealthiest king in the world because of his control over the gold trade. Mansa Musa would also travel, but this king traveled eastward to Mecca in Arabia on the Islamic holy pilgrimage named Hajj. When Mansa Musa arrived in Mecca, he met with the Arab historian and scholar Shihab Al-Umari, who was born in Damascus (modern-day Syria). Shihab Al-Umari quotes Mansa Musa as stating the following concerning his predecessor Mansa Abubakri II:

"We belong to a house which hands on the kingship by inheritance. The ruler who preceded me did not believe that it was impossible to reach the extremity of the ocean that encircles the earth and wanted to reach that (end) and obstinately persisted in the design. So he equipped two hundred boats full of men, full of gold, water, and victuals sufficient enough for several years. He ordered the admiral not to return until they had reached the extremity of the ocean, or if they had exhausted the provisions and the

water. They set out. Their absence extended over a long period, and at last, only one boat returned. On our questioning, the captain said: 'Prince, we had navigated for a long time until we saw in the midst of the ocean as if a big river was flowing violently. I sailed backward to escape this current.' But the Sultan would not believe him. He ordered two thousand boats to be equipped for him and for his men, and one thousand more for water and victuals. Then he conferred on me the regency during his absence and departed with his men on the ocean trip, never to return nor to give a sign of life. That was the last we saw of him and all those who were with him, and so I became king in my own right."

It is worth noting that just over 181 years later in AD 1492, an Italian explorer named Christopher Columbus would attempt a similar voyage toward the Americas—this time sailing from the European country of Spain. When Columbus reached the Americas, he was informed by the Native American tribes of the following: *"Black-skinned people have already come from the southeast in boats, trading in gold-tipped spears which they call guanin."* Christopher Columbus decided to verify what the Native Americans had told him about the African presence. He sent the spear points to the king and queen of Spain which were found to have thirty-two parts: eighteen of gold, six of silver, and eight of copper. It was found that the ratio of properties of gold, copper, and silver alloy was identical to the spears forged in western Africa. Columbus also noted that he saw natives with well-made multicolored scarves or sashes, which resembled West African sashes, one for the head and one for the rest of the body.

King John II of Portugal was the King of Portugal from AD 1481 until his death in AD 1495. According to the abstract of Christopher Columbus's log made by Bartolome de la Casas, the purpose of Christopher Columbus's third voyage was to test the claim of King John II of Portugal that "canoes had been found which set out from the coast of Guinea (West Africa) and sailed to the west (Americas) with merchandise." Bartolomé de las Casas was a Spanish landowner, priest, and historian born in AD 1484.

23

African in Mali on the Niger River

Indeed, two currents would have facilitated the voyage from West Africa to the Americas, and these were the Guinea Current and the Canary Current. Ocean currents are continuous, predictable, directional movements of seawater driven by gravity, wind, and temperature. Leveraging ocean currents facilitate traveling large distances. The Guinea Current is a slow warm water current that flows along the Guinea coast of West Africa. The Canary Current is a wind-driven surface current that flows from West Africa toward the Americas. Several experiments have concluded that the current can indeed easily carry a boat to the Americas such as one in AD 1971, conducted by the Norwegian ethnographer, Dr. Thor Heyerdahl. Dr. Thor Heyerdahl constructed a papyrus boat, and without the aid of modern boat technology and armed with only a small crew, it sailed from Africa to the Caribbean in fifty-seven days by leveraging the Canary Current. The experiment proved that virtually, any waterborne craft shoving off from the North Atlantic shores of Africa would inevitably enter the Caribbean. In essence, the Canary Current that flows from West Africa to the Americas would have facilitated travel from Africa to the Americas but prevented it in the opposite direction.

In AD 1513, a Spanish explorer named Vasco Nunez de Balboa also traveled to the Americas and, specifically, to Central and South America. He journeyed to the area, which is now modern-day Panama, and was also informed by the Native Americans that Africans were already present in the region and lived in the mountains and that they had been there for some time now. Vasco Núñez de Balboa also traveled to a village near Cuarecua in Panama and the Native Americans informed him of the following:

"There is a region only two days away where there are many Africans."

They also told him the following:

"These people came from Africa and were shipwrecked here, and they settled in the mountains and we sometimes war with them."

Mansa Abubakri II is remembered as a great traveler, pioneer, visionary, and brave leader of the empire. The next king in line would be the great and world-renowned Mansa Musa.

CHAPTER 6

Mansa Musa

Great Mosque of Djenné

After the previous ruler Mansa Abubakari II departed for his voyage to the Americas, Mansa Musa Keita I took his place as ruler. Mansa Musa Keita I came to power in AD 1312.

Mansa Musa was also known as "The Lion of Mali" and held other such titles, including "Lord of the Mines of Wangara" and "Conqueror of Ghanata." Mansa Musa in total conquered twenty-four cities, each with surrounding districts containing villages and estates, and, as a consequence, ruled over twenty-four lesser kings. Mansa Musa is also known in world history as the wealthiest man to have ever lived. He was also an extremely devout and pious Muslim. The capital of the empire at this time was still the city of Niani, which was very close to the gold-producing fields of Bambuk and Bure, near the upper Senegal River. By this time, Niani had a population of over twenty million people. The new king embarked on a campaign to eliminate the remaining bandits of the countryside, and soon, safety firmly established the efficiency of trade within the Mali Empire territory, was greatly increased.

Mansa Musa also developed strong ties with neighboring nations such as the Marinid Sultanate, located in northern Africa in modern-day Morocco. Now Abū al-Ḥasan ʿAlī was an African ruler of Morocco and part of the Marinid Sultanate. He was also known as the "Black Sultan" of Morocco. Abū al-Ḥasan ʿAlī's mother was from the nation of Ethiopia. Mansa Musa forged strong diplomatic and trade links with Abū al-Ḥasan ʿAlī and the Marinid Sultanate who sent gifts to the Mali Empire. The two African empires from that time onward sent envoys to each other and engaged in the exchange of gifts. As Mansa Musa was an extremely pious and observant Muslim, he further established Islam throughout the empire and used his immense wealth for the propagation of Islam. Under the leadership of Mansa Musa, the empire established ambassadors all across northern Africa, and the capital city of Mali was visited by Islamic scholars from many regions. He also encouraged Islamic scholarship by sending students from Mali to study in Fez in Morocco. Mansa Musa embarked on a large program of construction within the empire building universities and mosques in the city of Timbuktu to the east.

Clay Mosque, Djenne, Mali

He also constructed a grand royal palace for himself. In addition, he built the Hall of Audience in the city of Niani, where some of the finest examples of architectural expertise at the time were on display, and these included window frames of gold and silver, cut stone, wooden floors framed in silver foil, and adornments of arabesques (geometric patterns). In AD 1325, the army of Mali captured the city of Gao which was on the west bank of the Niger River. The city of Gao had previously been independent of the Mali Empire.

The Kingdom of Gao was one of the most powerful states in western Africa at the time, and therefore, the capture of the city was an important achievement for the Mali Empire. The successful operation was led by the Malian military general Sagmandia. At this time, the Mali Empire was equipped with an army numbering over one hundred thousand men, including an armored cavalry with ten thousand horses. The Kingdom of Gao measured several hundreds of miles across, so the conquest meant the acquisition of a vast territory. Ibn Battuta, an African Berber scholar and explorer, noted that it took about four months to travel from the northern borders of the Mali Empire to Niani in the south. The Mali Empire at this time controlled territory of vast proportions, making it the largest West African power at the time. The Mali Empire at this time controlled four hundred cities, towns, and villages in total. Mansa Musa embarked on a pilgrimage to the city of Mecca in Arabia in AD 1325, and this act would make him famous around the entire world. Mansa Musa consulted his diviners to learn the best date for his departure.

The Great Mosque of Djenné

The entire journey would take almost twelve months to complete. Mansa Musa traveled from Mali in the west, across to eastern Africa, and eventually into Arabia. The king took with him sixty thousand men, all wearing brocade and Persian silk, including twelve thousand servants, who each carried gold bars, and also one hundred camels who carried 135 kilos of gold dust each. The group also carried with them other goods and textiles. The king also traveled with one of his wives, who herself had hundreds of servants, as well as soldiers, merchants, court officials, and camel drivers.

Mansa Musa provided all necessities for the procession, feeding the entire group of men and animals for the duration of the journey. Mansa Musa soon arrived in the city of Cairo in Egypt and camped outside the pyramids, his presence causing a large amount of excitement among the locals. The Malians frequented the markets of Cairo, buying goods and gifts, and stunned the inhabitants with their sheer abundance of wealth. They stayed in Cairo for three months. Several eyewitness accounts at the time attest to the vast array of wealth that the king carried with him, and it is understood that he gave away so much gold to the poor during his journey that the sudden influx devastated the gold markets of Egypt, Medina, and Mecca for the next decade. For example, the value of the gold dinar in Cairo crashed by 20 percent. The gold dinar was an Islamic medieval gold coin used in trade. This was the only time one man controlled the price of gold across such a large region. Al-Makrizi, the Arab historian, provides the following description of the great Mansa Musa:

"He was a young looking man with brown skin, a pleasant face, and a good figure . . . His gifts amazed the eye with their beauty and splendor."

The Catalan Atlas was one of the most important geographical maps of Europe and developed in Europe's medieval period, it was drawn in AD 1375. By this time, the knowledge of the immense wealth of Mansa Musa had become so well-known around the world that the great African king is depicted on the Catalan Atlas holding large nuggets of West African gold. Mansa Musa's pilgrimage boosted Islamic education in Mali by adding mosques, libraries, and universities. The awareness of Mansa Musa by other Islamic leaders brought increased commerce and scholars, poets, and artisans, making the Malian city of Timbuktu one of the leading cities in the Islamic world. While in Mecca, Mansa Musa also convinced four shurafa to return with him to West Africa and reside within the empire.

The shurafa were direct descendants of the Prophet Muhammed, who was a key prophet in the religion of Islam. Abu Ishaq al-Sahili was a well-known Arab architect, scholar, and poet whom Mansa Musa also met while on his pilgrimage to Mecca. Mansa Musa commissioned Abu Ishaq al-Sahili to assist in the design and construction of several buildings for the Mali Empire, including the Djinguereber Mosque located in the city of Timbuktu. Musa's reign is commonly regarded as Mali Empire's golden age. Mansa Musa is remembered as the wealthiest man to have ever lived and ruled the Mali Empire for a total of twenty-five years. Mansa Musa is also credited with establishing Mali's reputation of greatness far beyond his imperial territories.

CHAPTER 7

Islam in Ancient Mali

African Muslim Reading the Quran

The Religion of Islam

The term Islam means "submission" or more specifically, "total submission to the will of God." The religion is one of the three Abrahamic religions, the other two being Judaism and Christianity. Islam was brought to Arabia by the Prophet Muhammed, although it is understood within the religion that Prophet Muhammed taught exactly the same message as all the prophets in the Abrahamic religion, including but not limited to Adam, Noah, Moses, Abraham, David, Solomon, and Jesus. Prophet Muhammed is considered to be the final prophet of God or the "seal of the prophets." Prophet Muhammed was an Arab who was born in Arabia in AD 570. The foundation of the religion included a total of six articles of faith, which all Muslims believe in. The articles of faith are (1) a belief in the existence of one God (also known as monotheism); (2) a belief in angels; (3) a belief in the existence of the books of God, which include the Quran, the Gospel, the Torah, and Psalms; (4) a belief in the prophets of God; (5) a belief in predestination; and (6) a belief in the Day of Judgment, which is a day in which all humans after death are judged based on their deeds and sent to either heaven (paradise) or hell (punishment).

The religion of Islam also includes five pillars or core beliefs: (1) the belief that "there is no god but God, and Muhammad is the Messenger of God" (this is also known as the declaration of faith or the Shahada); (2) prayer, in that Muslims pray facing Mecca in Arabia five times a day, and the times for prayer are at sunrise, noon, mid-afternoon, sunset, and night; (3) alms or zakat, which in Islamic law is the act of giving to the poor at least 2.5 percent of your wealth; (4) fasting during the daylight hours of Ramadan, which is the ninth month of the Islamic calendar and a holy month dedicated to prayer, reflection, and good deeds; and (5) Hajj, which is an annual Islamic pilgrimage to Mecca in Arabia (modern-day Saudi Arabia), the holiest city for Muslims. It is required for Muslims that can afford this, are physically able and are capable of supporting their family during their absence from home. This is performed at least once in their lifetime. The Prophet Muhammed, who was an Arab living in Arabia, received the Quran orally from God through the archangel Gabriel incrementally over some twenty-three years, beginning when Muhammad was forty years of age in AD 610. The Quran is considered the final book in a series of books of which God is the author.

The Introduction of Islam into Africa

The Prophet Muhammed first began the spread of the religion of Islam in Arabia, which is located east of the continent of Africa in modern-day Saudi Arabia in around AD 613, and he was successful in gaining significant followers. His early followers would come to include both Arabs and Africans, as well as Persians, Romans, and Jews. By AD 614, Muhammed and his followers were under significant attack and persecution by other groups within the region, including followers of polytheism and also members of the powerful Quraysh tribe of Arabia. At this time in eastern Africa, the Ethiopian Kingdom of Aksum had already been firmly established and, until AD 570, also controlled the territory of southern Arabia in the region of modern-day Yemen. Ethiopia was also known as Abyssinia at the time. In order to escape persecution, Muhammed and his followers contacted the leadership of Ethiopia for assistance. Under the instruction of Prophet Muhammed, the early followers of Islam fled from Arabia into eastern Africa. This was known as the First Hijrah. This was the first major introduction of Islam into the continent of Africa to a large degree. Following the death of Muhammed in AD 632, Islam spread into northern Africa.

The Byzantine Empire was first established in around AD 330 and was a continuation of the Roman Empire after the decline and eventual collapse of the western side of the Roman Empire, also known as the Western Roman Empire. The Byzantine Empire is also known as the Eastern Roman Empire or Byzantium. In AD 647, the Islamic Arabs launched a military campaign against the European Christian Byzantine Empire positions located in Egypt and, later, Carthage (located in modern-day Tunisia).

Ultimately, the Arabs were successful in defeating the Europeans, and as a consequence, the religion of Islam was slowly introduced to northern Africa. Populations of the region who were mostly African Berbers slowly began to convert to the new religion, and some mixing between to two cultures began to take place. The Berbers are an African ethnic group that has inhabited North Africa since 10,000 BC and are indigenous to the north African region—sometimes called the Maghreb. The Maghreb includes modern-day eastern Mauritania, western Sahara, Morocco, Algeria, Tunisia, Libya, northern Mali, and northern Niger. The Muslim Africans located in the north and northwest of the continent were also known collectively as "the Moors." In AD 711, an African Berber named Tariq ibn Ziyad, who was the governor of the Northwest African state of Mauritania, became commander of the military.

He would initiate the Moorish conquest of the European nation of Spain. Tariq ibn Ziyad led an army of seven thousand African soldiers and three hundred Arabs into southern Spain in the region known as Gibraltar, launching a full-scale invasion.

This would mark the beginning of a military campaign that would result in Spain being ruled by African Muslims and Arab Muslims for approximately 781 years. Following on from the conquest of southern Europe, the spread of Islam entered western Africa via merchants, traders, and scholars and was largely peaceful. First, it was adopted by African elites and then down into the wider population. In eastern Africa, Islam had already been introduced during the "First Hijrah" when the some early Muslims re-located to Ethiopia, but continued to expand via trade into the Swahili Coast by Muslim traders operating near the Red Sea, often existing alongside traditional African practices and rituals. The ease of adoption was facilitated both in the east of Africa and the west of Africa by the fact that trade and trust during trade were increased because merchants shared a set of beliefs. On the east coast, Muslim traders from Arabia and Egypt began to permanently settle in towns and trading centers along the Swahili coast. The local African peoples and Arabs mixed as did their languages, with intermarrying being common.

Mosque in Djenne

If the first large groups of Africans to adopt Islam were the merchants, then the second group were the courtiers and rulers themselves. On the west coast, among kingdoms (such as the Ghana Empire in the early days), Islam was tolerated, but the elite at first did not convert, preferring instead to continue with traditional African traditions and religions; however, this trend would change over time. Eventually, via increased trade, the religion spread across other regions of the African continent, gaining more popularity in the Kanem Empire and the Ghana Empire.

The Kanem Empire (also known as the Kanem–Bornu Empire) was first established in AD 700 in the area of North Central Africa, which covered the region of modern-day eastern Niger, western Chad, northeastern Nigeria, northern Cameroon, and southern Libya. Gradually, the religion of Islam came to have some influence in the royal court of the Kanem Empire, and an African queen named Queen Hawwa was the first member of the royal family to embrace and convert to Islam. In AD 1067, Queen Hawwa was established as the first Islamic ruler of the Kanem Empire and ruled for a total of four years.

The Ghana Empire was located in the modern-day southeast region of Mauritania and western Mali. Within the Ghana Empire, which was established in AD 800, the capital, which was Koumbi Saleh, was significantly divided into two distinct towns. One town was Muslim and boasted twelve mosques, while the other was the royal residence with many traditional cult shrines and only one mosque for visiting merchants. This division reflected the continuance of indigenous animist beliefs alongside Islam, the former being practiced by rural communities. By the time of the rise of the Mali Empire, however, Islam was more deeply embedded into the fabric of the empire.

African Muslim Reading the Quran

Islam in the Mali Empire

The first convert to Islam in the Mali Empire was the founder Sundiata, who practiced a loose form of Islam, often combining Islamic and indigenous western African beliefs. This was also the case for the majority of the population at the time, and generally, the leadership of the Mali Empire was usually strict Muslims.

The Malian king Mansa Uli, who was the second king, went on a pilgrimage to the holy city of Mecca in Arabia (modern-day Saudi Arabia), and he was the first ruler to do so, establishing the tradition. It was with the rise of Mansa Musa Keita I, who came to power in AD 1312, and the large increase in the quantity of trade and commercial activities that saw the explosion of Islam across the empire. African Muslim traders operated various trade networks across the empire and the surrounding regions, and with this, more and more of the population converted. Eventually, a class of learned West African scholars and clerics would be established, many of which studied in the North African city of Fez in Morocco. Muslim clerics often made themselves very useful to the community in practical daily life by offering prayers on request, offering medical advice, interpreting dreams, and performing administrative tasks. In Mali, an association with Islam sometimes brought a certain prestige to its adherents, and in addition, small changes in customs were observable such as modesty in the dress of women and the adoption of names associated with Islam, although they were usually blended with traditional West African names.

West African Muslims would find various ways to incorporate Islam and blend their traditional beliefs in other ways. For example, before the arrival of Islam in West Africa, women and children often wore amulets for protection. An amulet is a good luck charm, usually an object or piece of jewelry. With the arrival of Islam, this practice continued, but their amulets began to include Qur'anic verses or prayers. In this way, they managed to synchronize Islam with some of West Africa's indigenous beliefs. The introduction of Islamic law, also known as sharia, would also have some effects on life in Mali. The term "sharia" refers to God's immutable divine law. For example, many rural West African societies considered previously that land belonged to the community, while Islamic law emphasizes individual ownership of land.

New mosques in Gao, Djenne, and Timbuktu were constructed, as well as new courts of Islamic law. The Djinguereber Mosque in Timbuktu, Mali was a particularly famous learning center constructed in AD 1327. Knowledge was passed to the students through a sequence of teachers known as "silsila," which means link or chain in the Sufi tradition of Islam, which was very popular in West Africa at the time. The Sufi tradition is well-known in Africa as the mystical dimension of Islam, so the students would listen and learn from the sisila and write down the knowledge and study and understand its meaning. The religion of Islam is still heavily present in western Africa, and almost 50 percent of the population of the continent of Africa follows the religion of Islam in the present day.

CHAPTER 8

Architecture in the Mali Empire

The Great Mosque of Djenné, Mali

The Mali Empire was an extremely prosperous nation and, as a consequence, engaged in the development of numerous architectural projects, both large and small. Large constructions included palaces and mosques, and also smaller homes were built. The mosques were usually multistoried structures with towers, large wooden doors, and tiered minarets. The style of construction of the buildings in the Mali Empire was unique in that many of the larger buildings used wood logs that protruded from the walls. These wood logs ran through the buildings from one outer wall to the other and were used as support beams. They are sometimes known as "toron." In addition, these beams added a style that made the buildings more attractive and also had a practical use as scaffolding when doing repairs and modifications in the future. The style of building used by the Mali Empire is also known as Sudano-Sahelian architecture or Sahelian architecture.

Homes in the Mali Empire

For the majority of homes where families lived, the development of brick homes with flat roofs became widespread. The home builders would use mud blocks and short wooden branches. Typically, the homes were of a rectangular shape and were two stories tall.

The mud blocks were created by combining the mud with husks from grains. The mud blocks were then dried and left in the sun and used for building interior and exterior walls. Finally, a plaster made from earth and water was applied. The first floor of the homes was used to store goods and produce for trade and consumption, while the second floor was where the family resided. Many of these homes would be built by hand by groups of men and usually incorporated one or many windows. Some excavations in the Malian city of Niani have revealed the remains of houses and their stone foundations, confirming that more wealthy members of the empire built and lived in stone houses.

Djinguereber Mosque

The Djinguereber Mosque was located within the city of Timbuktu and constructed during the reign of Mansa Musa Keita I. Mansa Musa commissioned the architect Abu Ishaq al-Sahili to assist in the design of the Djinguereber Mosque; however, the style remained in accordance with typical West African building design styles.

The Djinguereber Mosque

The Djinguereber Mosque is constructed of mud blocks and includes three inner courts, two minarets, and twenty-five rows of pillars aligned in an east-west direction. The Djinguereber Mosque is one of the key mosques associated with the University of Timbuktu, the other two being the Sankore Mosque and the Sidi Yahya Mosque. The University of Timbuktu is one of Africa's oldest universities.

The Sidi Yahya Mosque

The Sidi Yahya Mosque was located south of the more famous Sankoré Mosque, which was located in modern-day Mali. Sidi Yahya operated as both a mosque and a madrassa. A madrassa is a type of Islamic educational institution. The doors of the mosque included beautiful designs, which make it unique. The structure includes wooden doors, a prayer hall, and arches. Also, a minaret is located above the courtyard. In addition, the imams of the mosque are buried in an underground location to the north of the structure.

The Sidi Yahya Mosque

The Great Mosque of Djenné

The Great Mosque of Djenné is located in the city of Djenne in modern-day Mali. The mosque is also the largest mud-built structure in the world. The façade of the Great Mosque of Djenné includes three minarets and a series of columns. The roof has several holes which provide its interior spaces with fresh air. The original mosque has been redeveloped in modern times. In typical Malian style, the mosque has hundreds of wood logs made from timber that protrude from the structure's walls. The large structure has large pillars and is topped with ostrich eggs, and the mosque's prayer hall can fit as many as three thousand people. The tombs of great regional scholars are adjacent to the mosque.

The Great Mosque of Djenné

The Sankore Mosque

The Sankore Mosque is also known as the University of Sankore and is one of the three mosques which make up the University of Timbuktu, located in modern-day Mali. The other two are Djinguereber and Sidi Yahya. The Sankore Mosque was modified during the rule of Mansa Musa Keita I. Again, in accord with the typical design of West African Sahelian architecture, a wooden framework was incorporated into the walls of the building. The Sankore Mosque was also used as a place of learning and features a large courtyard.

The Sankore Mosque

CHAPTER 9

The Trans-Saharan Trade Routes and
the Economy of the Mali Empire

The Sahara Desert

The Sahara region stretches from western Africa to eastern Africa and also encompasses much of northern Africa. In earlier years, the Sahara was a fertile region as depicted in African paintings from as early as 12,000 BC. The Sahara desert eventually covered a territory of over 3,600,000 square miles. Now, the trans-Saharan trade route refers to the interconnected set of trade routes that linked the African kingdoms and empires within the Sahara region. The Africans had established the trans-Saharan trade routes by AD 500, and from then onward, it simply expanded to encompass a greater and greater territory. The Ghana Empire was already established by AD 300, and the territory of the empire incapsulated modern-day Mali, southern Mauritania, and the area between the Niger and Senegal Rivers. By AD 770, the kings of the Ghana Empire had full control over the trade routes of the Sahara. The kingdom also benefited from its location, which was between the Senegal River and the Niger River. The empire became extremely wealthy because of the salt and gold trade between West Africa and North Africa. The water oasis dotted across the Sahara at the time provided resting and refueling places for the African traders.

Africans used caravans of camels to transport their goods to different nations and empires. The camel was domesticated and used to transport goods between the trading cities because of their inherent ability to travel long distances and carry up to three hundred kilograms of goods; In addition, camels were able to provide, milk, and meat, and camel skins were used for leather. Cowrie shells were introduced from the eastern coast as local currency and also kola nuts, but gold and salt remained the principal mediums of long-distance trade. These camel caravans ranged from one thousand up to twelve thousand camels in total. The trans-Saharan trade routes allowed Africans to transport goods such as salt, gold, copper, books, iron, kola nuts, fruits, linen, cloth, ivory, hides, ostrich feathers textiles, horses, glassware, weapons, sugar, cereals (sorghum and millet), spices, and beads and cowry shells. By AD 800, the Ghana Empire completely controlled the gold trade from Ghana to northern Africa, becoming extremely wealthy in the process.

The Sahara Desert

By AD 1000, the Ghana Empire had expanded its territory even farther west, past the Senegal River, farther south to the Bambuk region, farther east into the Niger, and north up to the Berber city of Audoghast. This expansion meant that the Ghana Empire now controlled a territory of 650,00 square kilometers, which is about double the size of modern-day Germany. The decline of the Ghana Empire in AD 1200 provided the growing Mali Empire with an opportunity to take over both the territory of the Ghana Empire and their influence over the trans-Saharan trade routes.

For the Mali Empire, both their adoption of Islam and the spread of Islam across western Africa and northern Africa increased the expansion and solidification of the trade routes. Islam ensured the establishment of common values and rules upon which trade could be conducted. Africans from various kingdoms and nations were more inclined to trust each other as they now shared a common belief system. As more African elites and royal families adopted the new religion, they, in turn, encouraged the local populations to do the same. This was done to help strengthen the networks of trade and ultimately increase the wealth of the kingdoms and empires involved.

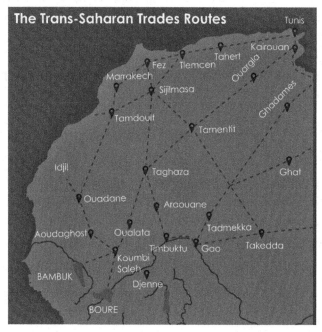

The Trans-Saharan Trade Routes

The Salt Trade

For the Mali Empire, the trade in salt was an extremely important commodity and source of income and wealth. The Taghaza region to the north of the empire continued to generate salt in abundance. Salt mines in Awlil and Idjil to the west of the empire were used. Salt was transported by both camel caravans and by boat along rivers such as the Senegal River and the Niger River. The cost of salt once transported to the capital of Mali was known to quadruple in price. Most commonly, salt was exchanged for gold and gold derivatives such as gold dust. Salt was used to preserve meat and also added to food for taste. With regard to salt, the demand usually outstripped the supply, which kept prices at a premium, and in many cases, it was exchanged directly for gold dust. In rural areas, salt could even be cut into small pieces and used as currency in some transactions. Large salt slabs were loaded onto camels, with each camel carrying two blocks, which weighed two hundred pounds each. A two-hundred-pound block of salt, transported by river from Timbuktu to Djenne in the south, could double its value and be worth around 450 grams of gold. When camel caravans arrived at a trading city, the salt was sold or exchanged for other valuable goods such as ivory, animal skins, and gold. The Malian city of Taghaza was so abundant in salt mines that it was known to have structures with walls and roofs constructed purely from salt.

The Copper Trade

Within the Mali Empire, the trade of copper flourished, and Mali expanded its production of copper from the mines of Takedda in the east of the kingdom and traded in the south of the kingdom. Takedda was located in present-day Niger.

The Gold Trade

Gold mined in Bambuk and Bure, as well as other sources, enabled the Mali Empire to produce almost half the gold in Africa. The currency or coinage of Mali was known as the mithqal or dinar and was equivalent to 4.5 grams of gold. From AD 1235, the great Mali Empire dominated the gold trade and established the trading centers of Timbuktu and Djenne. The gold fields of Bure and Bambuk provided a key source of gold for the Mali Empire and allowed them to generate considerable wealth. The Mali Empire was abundant in gold, so much so that it became world renowned, evidenced by the fact that Spanish maps from the year AD 1375 represented the king of Mali holding large nuggets of West African gold. Mali, by this time, had become much more international in trade than its predecessors, the Ghana Empire. The trade in gold also saw the rise of other powerful empires (such as the Kanem Empire), the expansion of cities (such as Kano), and the rise of powerful trading classes (such as the Wangara). The Wangara merchants formed an important trade diaspora for the Mali Empire, stretching from the region of modern-day Gambia in the west to Borno in the east; they also had connections across the Mali Empire and some of the Akan states on the southern Atlantic coast.

In North Africa, the city of Sijilmasa was located within the Berber kingdom of Morocco and had been founded in AD 757 by the African Berbers of the region, being one of the key North African cities that formed part of the trade routes. The city housed a population of thirty thousand people, and gold brought from western Africa within the territory of the Mali Empire was minted and traded there.

The following cities formed part of the trans-Saharan trades routes, which the Mali Empire was heavily involved with: Djenne, Timbuktu, Koumbi Saleh, Gao, Takedda, Tadmekka, Aoudaghost, Oualata, Ouadane, Idjil, Araouane, Taghaza, Ghat, Tamentit, Tamdoult, Sijilmasa, Ghadames, Ouargia, Kairouan, Tahert, Tlemcen, Njimi, Chinguetti, Fez, and Marrakech.

The Sahara Desert

Ibn Battuta was the North African Berber Muslim historian born in AD 1304, who traveled around north and western Africa and also to some of the cities that formed part of the trans-Saharan trade routes and the Mali Empire. Ibn Battuta wrote about the places he observed and the people he met during his travels. In his book *Travels in Asia and Africa*, Ibn Battuta provides an eyewitness account of what he observed. Ibn Battuta provides the following description of Taghaza located in modern-day northern Mali:

"After twenty-five days from Sijilmasa, we reached Taghaza. No one lives at Taghaza except the servants of the Massufa tribe who dig for the salt; they subsist on dates imported from Dar'a and Sijilmasa, camels' flesh, and millet imported from West Africa. The Malians come up from their country and take away the salt from there. At Walata, a load of salt brings eight to ten mithqals; in the territory of Mali, it sells for twenty to thirty and, sometimes, as much as forty. The Malians use salt as a medium of exchange, just as gold and silver are used elsewhere; they cut it up into pieces and buy and sell with it. The business done at Taghaza, for all its meanness, amounts to an enormous figure in terms of hundredweights of gold dust. We passed ten days of discomfort there. Water supplies are laid in at Taghaza for the crossing of

the desert which lies beyond it, which is a ten-night journey with no water on the way except on rare occasions.

We indeed had the good fortune to find water in plenty, in pools left by the rain. One day, we found a pool of sweet water between two rocky prominences. We quenched our thirst at it and then washed our clothes."

Marrakech was another city that formed part of the trans-Saharan trade routes. Ibn Battuta provides the following description of Marrakech located in modern-day Morocco:

"It is one of the most beautiful of cities, spaciously built and extending over a wide area, with abundant supplies. It contains magnificent mosques, such as its principal mosque, known as the Mosque of the Kutubiyin (the Bookseller). There is a marvelously tall minaret there; I climbed it and obtained a view of the whole town from it."

Also, the city of Timbuktu in Mali became the book trading center of the world at this time. From Timbuktu, trade took place across the Sahara near the town of Takedda (modern-day Niger), which was also later controlled by the Mali Empire. The city of Timbuktu contained copious sweet water wells as it had close proximity to the Niger River. A trade route from Takedda near the Tibesti Mountains (modern-day northern Chad), east to the city of Cairo, was created (modern-day Egypt). From the Hausa Kingdoms of western Africa (modern-day northern Nigeria), trade routes were established from their region to the capital city of the Kanem Empire called Njimi (modern-day Chad and Niger). In northern Africa, trade routes from Marrakesh (modern-day eastern Morocco) to Fez (modern-day northern Morocco) across to Kairouan (modern-day Tunisia) ending in Libya were created. Trade routes also expanded into the far east of Africa and into the lands of Ethiopia. All these routes enriched the Mali Empire and the traders that used them and supported not only the trade of goods but also the spread of knowledge.

Gold Nuggets

Shells were also a popular medium of exchange in the kingdom. Kola nuts were grown in the forests of Akan (modern-day Ghana), and thousands of tons of kola nuts were traded annually and also used in religious ceremonies such as marriages and name-giving ceremonies. The Niger River became significant in facilitating trade via the use of river boats. In addition, taxes were levied on all goods traded within the empire and paid to the kings and governors. The farmers of the empire were heavily engaged in agriculture and the growing of millet and the cultivation of rice and sorghum. In addition, fishing and the breeding of cattle were popular, and surplus was sold. Eventually, by the sixteenth century, the use of the trans-Saharan trade routes began to decline in usage in favor of other trade passages, but they are remembered as excellent examples of the effective spirit of coordination and cooperation that took place in western and northern Africa.

Gold Nuggets

CHAPTER 10

The City of Timbuktu

Doors in Timbuktu

The city of Timbuktu was already established in the West African region prior to the rise of the Mali Empire. Timbuktu was located in western Africa, in modern-day Mali, eight miles north of the Niger River. The city of Timbuktu was also one of the cities which formed the series of trading centers that formed part of the trans-Saharan trade routes along with others such as Tadmekka, Gao, Takedda, Djenne, Aoudaghost, Oualata, and Araouane. To the east of Timbuktu was the Malian-controlled city of Koumbi Saleh, to the east was the Malian city of Gao, and to the south was the city of Djenne. Timbuktu was a center of scholarship under several African empires; the city rose to become one of the premier centers for knowledge and trade in the continent of Africa and indeed the world at that time under the Mali Empire. The city was able to act as somewhat of a middle ground in the exchange of goods between North African cities and West African cities.

Timbuktu was the starting point for trans-Saharan camel caravans which transported goods northward toward African Berber territory. As a consequence, the city itself had a variety of different African groups living within it, including the Mandinka, Fulani, African Berbers, Songhai, Wangara, Tuareg, Arabs, and other West African groups.

Being part of the network of cities within the trans-Saharan trade routes meant that goods such as salt, gold, copper, books, iron, kola nuts, fruits, linen, cloth, ivory, hides, ostrich feathers textiles, horses, glassware, weapons, sugar, cereals (sorghum and millet), spices, beads, and cowry shells were exchanged there, although Timbuktu would become synonymous with book trading. The city was overseen by a regional governor appointed by the king who was responsible for managing the growing population of tens of thousands, imposing taxes on trade, settling disputes, dispensing justice, and maintaining law, order, and security. By AD 1235, the Mali Empire took control over the city of Timbuktu. The Malian king Mansa Musa constructed one of his royal palaces in the city, and the city flourished under his rule.

Timbuktu, Mali

Timbuktu as the Center of Learning

Timbuktu became a place where many of the premier Islamic scholars from Bagdad in Iraq, Cairo in Egypt, and Persia (modern-day Iran) came to learn and teach; it was also home to several hundred thousand manuscripts. Many travelers to and from the city noted the thirst for books and knowledge there. The profit made by buying and selling books was only second to the gold-salt trade. Indeed, the universities of Fez in Morocco and the University of Timbuktu, which included the Sankore Mosque, were said to be equals. Furthermore, commentaries written on the Quran were used in Jeddah, Arabia (modern-day Saudi Arabia) and Cairo, Egypt (modern-day Egypt).

Books were also imported from other regions, such Fez in modern-day Morocco, Cairo in modern- day Egypt, Tripoli in modern-day Libya, and Córdoba in modern-day southern Spain. The Malian king Mansa Musa constructed the three great mosques and madrasas of Mali named Sidi Yahya, Djinguereber Mosque, and the Sankore Mosque (also known as the Sankore Madrasah)—all of which combine to form part of the University of Timbuktu, which is still operational to the present day. Although all forms of goods and services were traded within Timbuktu, the most popular items were books because of a large number of schools within the city. Timbuktu had become the de facto headquarters of Islamic intellectual development in Africa. Scholars and students came from far and wide to learn the Quran and Islamic theology at the University of Timbuktu and covered topics such as law, grammar, rhetoric, logic, history, geography, astronomy, astrology, mathematics, medicine, and law. The Sankore Mosque and university consisted of numerous buildings, and each one was run by its own Islamic scholar. Classes were conducted in private rooms or within the open courtyards. The students used locally-made wooden boards and ink to complete assignments. Prior to entering the university, the students typically pursued two degrees. The first degree required learning how to read and write in Arabic.

The students admitted to the university then studied language, poetry, grammar, and literature for the second degree. There were both mandatory and optional studies. Mandatory studies included advanced grammar, philosophy, Islamic law, interpretation of the Quran, and language studies. Optional studies included algebra, medicine, chemistry, history, arithmetic, physics, and astronomy. In addition, the students were also reported to have spent time learning trades along with relevant business codes and ethics. The university trade shops offered classes in business, construction, shoe making, tailoring, navigation, carpentry, farming, and fishing. By AD 1400, the University of Timbuktu and private households in Timbuktu had one of the largest collections of books in Africa with over seven hundred thousand books within their possession.

By AD 1450, the population of the city of Timbuktu had swelled to over one hundred thousand inhabitants and over 180 Quranic schools with over twenty-five thousand students and scholars. The combination of Timbuktu's three main mosques, Islamic schools, universities, and scholarly classes meant that it became one of the holiest and most famous cities in the West African region. The explorer Ibn Battuta provides the following description concerning his travels to the city of Timbuktu:

"Timbuktu . . . is four miles from the Niger River. Most of its inhabitants are Massufa, people of the veil. Its governor . . . called Farba Musa . . . appointed one of the Massufa as amir over a company . . . placed on him a garment, a turban and trousers, all of them of dyed material. He then seated him on a shield and he was lifted up by the elders of his tribe on their heads . . . At Timbuktu, I embarked on the Niger in a small vessel carved from one piece of wood. We used to come ashore every night in a village to buy what we needed of food and in exchange for salt and perfumes and glass ornaments."

The city of Timbuktu produced some well-known scholars such as Sharif Sidi Yahya al-Tadilsi, who became the patron saint of the city. Another was Mohammed Bagayogo, who was born in Timbuktu and was a professor and teacher at the Sankore Madrasah. Modibo Mohammed Al Kaburi was another esteemed scholar of Timbuktu who was of Fulani descent, and he was also a jurist and professor.

Al-Qadi Aqib ibn Mahmud ibn Umar was a judge in the city of Timbuktu and imam of the Sankore Mosque. Ahmad Baba was born in the city of Araouane and also became a well-known scholar in Timbuktu. He moved to Timbuktu at an early age to study with his father and studied under other scholars also. Ahmad Baba was a chancellor of the University of Sankore and a prolific writer producing over forty books. He wrote books on astronomy, ethnography, and theology and developed a personal library with over 1,600 books.

Quran from Timbuktu

The Timbuktu Manuscripts

The Timbuktu Manuscripts refer to the extremely large quantity of books in the possession of both the University of Timbuktu and private households and libraries in Timbuktu, which totaled to more than seven hundred thousand books. Many of the books were written by hand by West Africans in the Songhai and Tamasheq languages. The Songhai language was used in western Africa, and Tamasheq was used in the west and also parts of northern Africa. In addition, many of the manuscripts were written in Arabic. The topics covered within these books included but were not limited to art, mathematics, astronomy, science, philosophy, Islamic law, Sufism, sociology, ophthalmology and other health matters, and the study of the Quran. All of these manuscripts were written primarily by West African scholars, scientists, historians, philosophers of the time, and the inhabitants of the city of Timbuktu.

Many works concerning Islamic jurisprudence, also known as "fiqh," were included in the writing. Islamic jurisprudence is concerned with the deep understanding of matters, especially those related to the religion of Islam and Islamic law. Along with Islamic jurisprudence were collections of hadiths. Hadiths refer to any of the various collected accountings of the words, actions, and habits of the Prophet Mohammad during his lifetime. Also among the manuscripts were diaries, dictionaries, letters between rulers and subjects, and legal opinions on coinage, marriage, and divorce. It was also commonplace for Muslims from other parts of Africa such as Egypt and Morocco to visit or relocate to Timbuktu, and in addition, Malian scholars would also travel and teach in both Morocco and Egypt and engage in writing. There were similar collections of libraries in the West African region such as the Libraries of Chinguetti, located in modern-day northern Mauritania; however, their book collections were not comparable to the scale present in the city of Timbuktu. A famous West African proverb states the following:

"Salt comes from the north, gold from the south, but the word of God and the treasures of wisdom come from Timbuktu."

The manuscripts represented the long legacy of written knowledge and academic excellence in Africa.

Timbuktu Manuscripts from Mali

The number of books in Timbuktu was extremely large because of the fact that it was a center of the manuscript trade, with traders bringing Islamic texts from all over the Muslim world.

In addition, we find within the texts several references to the presence of pre-Islamic poets, as well as full copies of the Quran showcasing the variety and breadth of the manuscripts.

The trade in these books with Timbuktu as the center is sometimes referred to as the African Ink Road. The African Ink Road describes the network of book trading activity and exchange of knowledge that connected north, west, and eastern Africa.

The Timbuktu Manuscripts benefited from the local class of artisans who scribed, decorated, and bound them, supporting the sophisticated book production industry. The books were often bound in leather and contained finely articulated calligraphy and colorful illustrations, and some books were gilded in addition. There developed a supporting industry around books which incorporated book copying, the paper trade, ink making, and binding.

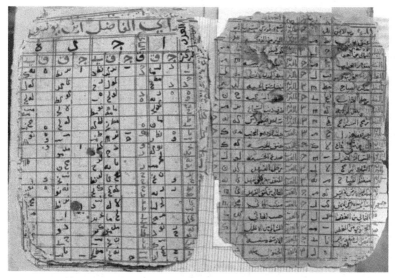

Timbuktu Manuscripts from Mali

Similar to the collections of books within the universities, individual scholars and wealthy scholarly families developed their own collections, which included both the original works and copied versions created by specialized scribes within the community. Book copying, when it took place, was extensive and well structured. At the end of a book, the title and author were clearly stated along with the names of the scribes who had produced it. In addition, they would sometimes mention for whom the manuscript was being copied, who provided the paper, and the money paid for the copy.

The manuscripts themselves ranged from one full page fragments to over 450 pages in length generally. Among the manuscripts found are legal documents such as contracts. These legal documents usually included a declaration concerning the validity of the contract, confirming that the parties involved were legally competent, free from restraint, and in full possession of their faculties. The legal document also stated clearly that they were lawful according to Islamic law, also known as "sharia." Finally, each legal document would end with the phrase, *"Praise to God and blessings upon the Prophet."*

Timbuktu Manuscript named: The Important Stars Among the Multitude of the Heavens

The manuscripts also included commercial documents used in business transactions, which usually started with the phrase, "Let all who read this document know." The manuscripts usually then went on to describe the name of the buyer and the seller of the commodity. A full description of the commodity and a declaration of the legal validity of the sale was also provided. Finally, a confirmation that the buyer paid the price in full and the name of the drafter and the date were provided.

CHAPTER 11

Accounts of the Mali Empire by Ibn Battuta

Mosque Mali, Djenne

Ibn Battuta was an African Berber who was born in AD 1304 in Morocco in North Africa. He was born into a family of Islamic legal scholars. Specifically, Ibn Battuta was born in the city of Tangier, located in modern-day Morocco, which is forty-five miles west of the Mediterranean Sea. Ibn Battuta is also known by his full name Abu Abdullah Muhammad Ibn Battuta. His family belonged to a North African Berber tribe known as the *Lawata*, which was part of the large and renowned Zenata Berber confederation. Ibn Battuta visited the Mali Empire as part of his travels around Africa and Asia and documented traveling to the Malian city of Oualata, which is also known as Walata. Oualata was located in modern-day Mauritania in western Africa.

The city was northwest of the city of Timbuktu and the Niger River. Concerning Oualata Ibn Battuta provides the following account:

"When I decided to make the journey to Mali, which is reached in twenty-four days from Walata if the traveler pushes on rapidly, I hired a guide from the Massufa, for there is no necessity to travel in a company on account of the safety of that road and set out with three of my companions.

A traveler in this country carries no provisions, whether plain food or seasonings, and neither good nor silver. He takes nothing but pieces of salt and glass ornaments, which the people call beads, and some aromatic goods. When he comes to a village the womenfolk of the West Africans bring out millet, milk, chickens, pulped lotus fruit, rice, 'funi' (a grain resembling mustard seed, from which couscous and gruel are made), and pounded haricot beans."

Mosque in Djenne, Mali

Ibn Battuta traveled through the territory of the Mali Empire and eventually reached the Niger River. He mentions both the Malian towns of Zagha and Kabara. He also mentions the Malian city of Gao, also known as Gawgaw. Ibn Battuta provides the following description concerning it:

"The Niger flows from there down to Kabara, and thence to Zagha. In both Kabara and Zagha, there are sultans who owe allegiance to the king of Mali. The inhabitants of Zagha are of old standing in Islam; they show great devotion and zeal for study. Thence the Niger descends to Timbuktu and Gawgaw, both of which will be described later; then to the town of Muli in the land of the Limis, which is the frontier province of the kingdom of Mali; thence to Yufi, one of the largest towns of the West Africans, whose ruler is one of the most considerable of the West African rulers. It cannot be visited by any white man because they would kill him before he got there."

Ibn Battuta traveled deeper into the Mali Empire, eventually reaching one of its central cities. However, he is not clear on which city. Nevertheless, Ibn Battuta provides the following description:

"Thus I reached the city of Mali, the capital of the king of the Malians. I met the qadi of Mali, 'Abd ar- Rahman, who came to see me; he is a West African, a pilgrim, and a man of fine character. I met also the interpreter Dugha, who is one of the principal men among the West Africans. All these persons sent me hospitality gifts of food and treated me with the utmost generosity—may God reward them for their kindnesses."

Ibn Battuta also had the good fortune to meet with the current Malian ruler and describes his experience in the following account:

"The sultan of Mali is Mansa Sulayman, 'mansa' meaning (in Mandinka) sultan and Sulayman being his proper name. It happened that I spent these two months without seeing him, on account of my illness. Later on, he held a banquet in commemoration of our master (the late sultan of Morocco) Abu'l- Hasan, to which the commanders, doctors, qadi, and preacher were invited, and I went along with them. Reading desks were brought in, and the Quran was read through, then they prayed for our master Abu'l-Hasan and also for Mansa Sulayman. When the ceremony was over, I went forward and saluted Mansa Sulayman. The qadi, the preacher, and Ibn al-Faqih told him who I was, and he answered them in their tongue. They said to me: The sultan says to you, 'Give thanks to God.' So I said, 'Praise be to God and thanks under all circumstances.' When I withdrew, the (sultan's) hospitality gift was sent to me."

Sirimou, Bozo Village, Mali

Ibn Battuta had the good fortune to witness some of the celebrations within the Mali Empire and provides the following commentary:

"The Mansa holds sessions during the days associated with the two festivals after the asr (later afternoon) prayers on the platform. The men at arms come with wonderful weaponry, quivers of silver and gold, swords covered with gold, their sheaths of the same, spears of silver and gold, and wands of crystal. Four of the amirs stand behind him to drive off flies, with ornaments of silver in their hands which look like riding stirrups. The farariyya (commanders), the qadi (judge), and the preacher sit according to custom, and the interpreter Dugha brings in his (the Mansa's) four wives and his concubines, who are about a hundred in number. On them are fine clothes, and on their heads, they have bands of silver and gold with silver and gold apples as pendants. A chair is set there for Dugha to sit on, and he beats an instrument which is made of reeds with tiny calabashes below it, praising the sultan, recalling in his song his expeditions and deeds."

Mali, Djenne

Ibn Battuta then provides his evaluation of the people of Mali.

"The Malians possess some admirable qualities. They are seldom unjust and have a greater abhorrence of injustice than any other people. Their sultan shows no mercy to anyone who is guilty of the least act of it. There is complete security in their country. Neither traveler nor inhabitant in it has anything to fear from robbers or men of violence."

"On Fridays, if a man does not go early to the mosque, he cannot find a corner to pray in, on account of the crowd. It is a custom of theirs to send each man his boy [to the mosque] with his prayer mat; the boy spreads it out for his master in a place befitting him [and remains on it] until he comes to the mosque. Their prayer mats are made of the leaves of a tree resembling a date palm but without fruit. Another of their good qualities is their habit of wearing clean white garments on Fridays. Even if a man has nothing but an old worn shirt, he washes it and cleans it and wears it to the Friday service. Yet another is their zeal for learning the Quran by heart."

Quran

Finally, Ibn Battuta provides a description of his travels to the city of Timbuktu:

"Then we went on to Timbuktu, which stands four miles from the River Niger. Most of its inhabitants are of the Massufa tribe, wearers of the face veil. Its governor is called Farba Musa. I was present with him one day when he had just appointed one of the Massufa to be the emir of a section. He assigned to him a robe, a turban, and trousers, all of them of dyed cloth, and bade him sit upon a shield, and the chiefs of his tribe raised him on their heads. In this town is the grave of the meritorious poet Abu Ishaq as-Sahili, of Granada, who is known in his own land as at-Tuwayjin. From Timbuktu, I sailed down the Niger River on a small boat, hollowed out of a single piece of wood. I went on to Gao, which is a large city on the Niger River, and one of the finest towns in Sudan. It is also one of their biggest and best-provisioned towns, with rice in plenty, milk, and fish, and there is a species of cucumber there called 'inani' which has no equal. The buying and selling of its inhabitants are done with cowrie shells, and the same is the case at Niani. I stayed there about a month, and then set out in the direction of Takadda by land with a large caravan of merchants from Ghadamis."

CHAPTER 12

The Griot

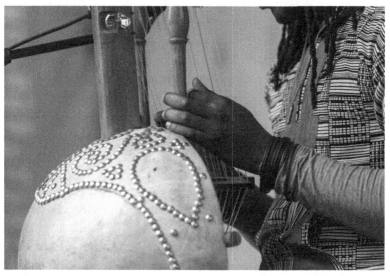

A West African Griot

In western Africa, since the founding of the great Mali Empire in AD 1235, the griot has been a key component of the culture within the empire. A griot is a West African historian, storyteller, poet, singer, and musician. The griots were extremely prevalent across the Mali Empire. The griot was also known across western Africa as the "jali" or "kewel." These griots would tell stories of well-known West African kings and queens, famous heroes, and legendary characters and were responsible for retaining and conveying history and legends to the general populous. Within the Mali Empire, various castes performed specific services or had particular skills in which they specialized, and the griots were no different in this regard. Griots were their own social caste, and there were also griot families, whereby the position was passed down from generation to generation. Members of the royal families and the elite of Mali would typically all have griots assigned to them, and villages would have griots assigned to them as well. For young griots, the training would start from as young as seven years old until the child had mastered the skills required and became an adult man or woman. Many of the stories of the griots were used to illustrate moral messages and to provide guidance in order to increase the strength and cohesiveness of the requisite villages under their jurisdiction. For Malians, histories of various groups were memorized and conveyed by the griot, as well as stories for the children of the villages and towns. Traditionally, most griots were men, but there were also some female griots who were known for their beautiful voices and specialized in singing as well as poetry.

Griots often also served as mediators between village inhabitants whenever issues or disagreements arose, and they provided wise counsel to both sides until a satisfactory resolution could be secured. Typically, each large village within the Mali Empire would have its own griot assigned to them. Some griots could tell the ancestry of every villager going back centuries and could speak continuously for many hours and, sometimes, even days. The role of the griot in the Malian Empire was often times hereditary, and many griots were also trained to play the "kora." The Mandinka ethnic group developed the kora, which is a West African musical instrument. Specifically, the kora is a long-necked harp lute typically constructed from a calabash. A calabash is a fruit that is produced by the calabash tree. The tree produces large spherical fruits that are usually twenty inches in diameter.

Calabash Tree

The shells were typically used by Malians to create bowls and also the kora instrument. The kora has twenty-one strings, with each one playing a different note, and the sound of a kora resembles that of a harp. Storytelling by the griot is often accompanied by the playing of the kora. The griots also used other instruments such as the "balafon." The balafon is a gourd-resonated xylophone. A balafon can be either fixed-key, where the keys are strung over a fixed frame, usually with calabash resonators underneath, or free-key, where the keys are placed independently on any padded surface.

The balafon usually has seventeen to twenty-one keys. The griot also uses the "ngoni." The ngoni is a small lute; it is a string instrument, a traditional guitar from the region of ancient Mali. The body of the ngoni is made of wood or calabash with dried animal skin stretched over it.

West African Griot Playing a Kora

The use of the ngoni was witnessed by the North African traveler Ibn Battuta during his visit to the royal court of the Mali Empire. In AD 1352, when Ibn Battuta arrived in Mali, a griot detailed some of the histories of Mali to him as the griot was also fluent in multiple languages including but not limited to Arabic. In addition, to serving as the historians and storytellers of their people, griots have also served West African kings and rulers as diplomats and advisers. Griots traditionally, at the request of the royal families, would tell stories of famous battles, marriages, achievements of individuals and groups, spiritual matters, and traditions. Within the Mali Empire, every royal family had a griot or group of griots assigned to them who would be responsible for the collection and communication of knowledge via poems, songs, speeches, history, and stories of the empire. Such close proximity to the elite allowed the griots to become wealthy in many instances and also to have a high degree of influence within society. Lengthy stories were sometimes recited as poems by the griots. Long West African poems such as these are sometimes referred to as an "epic." Another famous

West African story told by griots is the *Epic of Sundiata*, which details the founding of the Mali Empire. The Epic of Sundiata tells the story of the rise of King Sundiata and the creation of the Mali Empire. Within the story, Sundiata himself is assigned a griot by his parents, whereby the griot was to provide guidance and wisdom to him. Griots are present all over Africa and the world to the present day.

West African Griot Playing a Kora

CHAPTER 13

The Wangara

Gold Nuggets

The Mali Empire became one of the most prosperous and wealthy empires in the history of West Africa primarily because of its mastery of trade and commerce. A key component of this success was its ability to capitalize on the skills of the various guilds, classes, and social groups that made up the populous of the region. Indeed, it was not uncommon within West African empires and kingdoms to create societies and guilds with a specific focus, for example, guilds of astronomers, craftsmen, sculptors, griots, medicine men, and in the case of the Wangara, merchants. In western Africa, the Wangara was and is a merchant class that developed a series of sophisticated trade networks across western Africa. The Wangara descended from the Soninke ethnic group of

West Africa which was located in the modern-day countries of Senegal, southern Mauritania, the Gambia, Mali, and Guinea. The Soninke is a branch of the Mande people of West Africa just like the Mandinka. The Wangara is also known as the Soninke Wangara.

The Soninke speak their own language, which is also known as "serakhulle," and it is one of the Mande family of languages that were used throughout western Africa. The Soninke was also the ethnic group that founded the Ghana Empire in AD 300. The Wangara was also known as the "wakoré" or "ouankri" and originally followed local Soninke religions, which included a belief in one God and also in spirit beings. The Wangara merchants built a vast regional economic network, extending from the Sahel in the north to the Akan Forests in the south, then from the region which is modern-day Senegambia in the west across to the region which is modern-day western Nigeria in the east. Dating back to the founding of the Ghana Empire in AD 300, the Wangara was given specific privileges with regard to the trading of gold and gold derivatives. It is worth noting that the Wangara continued to operate throughout the duration of the Ghana Empire and into the time of the establishment of the Mali Empire in AD 1235. As the Ghana Empire declined, the Wangara had to now engage with the Mali Empire. Just as the Mali Empire adopted Islam by AD 800, so did the Wangara. The Wangara is also often associated with the "Dyula," which was another West African trading class located more to the east of the region. Among the Dyula, there was a scholarly class known as the "karamogo", who were known as wise men, teachers, and learned men. The characteristics which identify both groups were that they were West African, gold miners, gold traders, and Muslims. The Wangara became famous for their enterprise and skill and enjoyed a privileged position. The relationship was mutually beneficial in that the Mali Empire required gold and the Wangara became a major source.

Gold Nuggets

The Wangara, in turn, needed a market for their products. Therefore, the Wangara class of merchants became an important component of the Mali Empire. They were able to keep the prices of gold high via quantity restrictions and the control of gold mining activities, and they also engaged in the trade of gold dust. Gold dust (a gold derivative) was carefully measured out, typically using glass weights and small scales, and was used as a currency in some states. Being a wealthy merchant class also provided the Wangara access to high levels of education, and over time their group also included Islamic scholars, writers, and legal experts. All this trade and activity ensured that the Mali Empire at this time became the largest producer of gold in the world, and they went on to solidify the trans-Saharan gold trade in the region, becoming extremely wealthy in the process. Once the Wangara trading class had helped to facilitate the creation of the trans-Saharan gold trade routes in conjunction and collaboration with the Mali Empire, the region in general increased immensely in prosperity. Key sources of gold mining for the Wangara included the Bambuk and Bure goldfields near modern-day Gambia and the Akan goldfields located in modern-day Ghana. Trade and trust between the Wangara and the African Berbers of the north were also simplified by the fact that they shared the same religion, namely Islam. The oasis city of Sijilmasa located in Morocco just south of the Atlas Mountains served as a trading center for the Berbers and the Wangara. Soon, a mint was established there. A large area surrounding the city was walled using stone and brick, and twelve gates were constructed to enter it. Ahmad al-Ya'qubi was an Arab geographer who was born in Bagdad in the region of modern-day Iraq. Ahmad al-Ya'qubi provides the following description of the city:

"Around Sijilmasa, there are deposits of gold and silver. It is found like plants, and it is said that the wind blows it away."

This also provided the Wangara business opportunities to expand not just into North African markets and east into the African city of Egypt but also into Europe. Once gold was melted down and cast into gold bars, camels were used for its transportation. The gold coinage of the Mediterranean and Europe was sourced primarily from the Wangara gold merchants of West Africa. In addition, gold was used in the creation of jewelry, embroidered clothing, and even manuscripts. They remained the most enterprising and successful merchants of the region, traveling far and wide across deserts, plains, and forests. At this time, the Malian city of Djenne and the city of Timbuktu, already known for book trading, increasingly became important commercial centers for the gold trade and flourished. Djenne, which was southwest of Timbuktu, acted as an important connector between the southern forests and the east of the region. The magnitude of gold produced at this time reached tons every year. The Moroccan traveler Ibn Battuta, upon his travels to western Africa and the Mali Empire, provides the following account concerning the Wangara:

"After a distance of ten days' travel from Walata, we arrived at the village of Zaghari, which is a big place with black merchants living in it. They are called the Wangara."

Muhammad Al-Idrisi was a Muslim geographer and cartographer born in the region of modern-day Morocco in North Africa.

Muhammed Al-Idrisi described the towns of the Wangara in the following way:

"They have flourishing towns and famous strongholds. Its inhabitants are rich, for they possess gold in abundance, and many good things are imported to them from the outermost parts of the earth."

In order to help facilitate their trading activities, the Wangara merchants established rest stations along their trade routes which were called "ribats," an Arabic term for a small fortification. One such ribat that grew into a small commercial area was the town Bijini, located in the region of modern-day Guinea-Bissau. The influence of these Mande traders became so influential that the Mande languages became commonplace and the preferred mode of communication for trade in the region in a similar fashion to Arabic. The Wangara were also known to expand their commercial activities beyond the gold trade into other areas, including but not limited to agriculture and the manufacturing of footwear, talismans, and weapons. The trading activities and dominance of the Wanagra merchant class continued beyond the Mali Empire and well into the seventeenth century.

Gold Nuggets

CHAPTER 14

The Mali Empire King List

Mud Brick Mosque in Saba, Mali

Concerning the Mali Empire, historians have recorded a total of twenty-three kings of Mali from the time of the founder King Sundiata Keita; however, we know that there were several kings before the official founding of the empire during the time of the Kingdom of Kangara. The following kings or Mansa's ruled Mali from AD 1235:

Mansa Sundiata Keita: AD 1235
Mansa Sundiata was the founder of the Mali Empire. The famous Malian account named the *Epic of Sundiata* records how he conquered the ruler of the Susu, Sumanguru to establish the empire after the Battle of Kirina.

Mansa Uli Keita: AD 1255
Mansa Keita was the son of Mansa Sundiata Keita and was instrumental in increasing agricultural production across the nation. Mansa Uli Keita extended the territory to the north and added to the empire the trading centers of Walata and Timbuktu. Mansa Uli traveled to Mecca in Arabia for Hajj (the Islamic pilgrimage).

Mansa Wati Keita: AD 1270
Mansa Wati Keita was the third ruler of the empire, being adopted as a child by Mansa Sundiata Keita. He passed power on to his brother Mansa Khalifa in AD 1274.

Mansa Khalifa Keita: AD 1274
Mansa Khalifa Keita ruled for a short period and was not a popular leader among his people and was known for firing arrows at his subjects unjustly. His own people decided that he needed to be removed, and he was swiftly succeeded by Mansa Abubakari.

Mosque in Mopti, Mali

Mansa Abubakari Keita: AD 1275
Mansa Abubakari Keita ruled from AD 1275 until AD 1285 and was the uncle of Mansa Khalifa Keita. Mansa Abubakari was instrumental in returning the management of the empire back to a high level.

Mansa Sakura: AD 1285
Mansa Sakura was the only king of Mali not to be from the royal bloodline and was a servant in his early years. However, it was customary in western Africa for some servants to rise into higher positions over time, and in the case of Sakura, he became a general in the army of the Mali Empire. Mansa Sakura also conquered Gao in eastern Mali, bringing it under the umbrella of the empire. Further expansion was made into the neighboring region of modern-day Senegal, and he conquered the Wolof province named Dyolof. Mansa Sakura also went to Mecca for Hajj in Arabia but was killed on his way back by armed robbers.

Mansa Gao Keita: AD 1300
Mansa Gao Keita was directly related to Sundiata Keita's sister, making him a nephew of Sundiata.

Mansa Muhammed ibn Gao Keita: AD 1305
Mansa Muhammed ibn Gao Keita was the son of Mansa Gao Keita and ruled for five years, increasing the stability of the empire.

Mansa Abubakari Keita II: AD 1310
Mansa Abubakari Keita II (also known as Abu Bakr II) was a great explorer who abdicated his throne to traverse the Atlantic Ocean, organizing a large seafaring expedition. Some of the members returned to Mali to communicate their findings. Based on the reports of his captains, Mansa Abubakari Keita II later sailed himself to the Americas with a fleet of two thousand vessels, reaching there almost two hundred years before the European explorer Christopher Columbus later in AD 1492. Mansa Abubakari Keita II's fleet is thought to have eventually sailed into the region of modern-day Brazil in South America.

Mansa Musa I Keita: AD 1312

Mansa was the tenth and one of the most well-known kings of the Mali Empire. Mansa Musa took the throne after Mansa Abubakari Keita II and was a devout Muslim who engaged in the propagation of Islam throughout the empire and its surrounding areas. Mansa Musa, I, was also the wealthiest king to ever rule on earth as recognized by historical records. Mansa Musa invited scholars from around the Muslim world to Mali and constructed palaces and mosques in Gao, Niani, and Timbuktu. Under Mansa Musa's leadership, the Mali Empire became one of the largest and most powerful empires in the world at that time.

Mansa Meghan Keita I: AD 1337

Mansa Meghan was one of Musa I's younger sons and inherited the throne from him ahead of his older brother. The wealth of the empire continued to expand under his reign, and he ruled Mali for four years in total before passing on the leadership to his brother Suleiman Keita. Mansa Meghan also had several sons who would rule after him.

Mansa Suleiman Keita: AD 1341

Mansa Suleiman is credited with having a long reign of twenty-four years after inheriting the throne from his younger brother, Mansa Meghan. Mansa Suleiman had to fend off attacks from the neighboring Fula tribes and did so successfully. During this time, the North African Berber historian named Ibn Battuta visited Mali and wrote his account in the manuscript titled, "A Masterpiece to Those Who Contemplate the Wonders of Cities and the Marvels of Travelling." It is also known as "The Rihla."

Mansa Keita: AD 1360

The son of Mansa Suleyman ruled for less than one year and was defeated by his rival, Mari Djata, in an internal battle.

Mansa Mari Djata Keita II: AD 1360

Mansa Amri Djata was known for cultivating a relationship with the court of Morocco in northern Africa, sending them a giraffe, and also with the Northeast African court of Egypt. Mari Djata was also known for his extravagant spending.

Mansa Musa Keita II: AD 1374

Mansa Musa rose to power and focused his energies on redressing some of the excessive spendings of his predecessor.

Mansa Maghan Keita II: AD 1387

Mansa Maghan was another son of Maghan Keita II and reigned for two years before being succeeded by Sandaki.

Mansa Sandaki Keita: AD 1389 and Mansa Maghan Keita III: AD 1390

Mansa Sandaki was a relative of Mansa Mari Djata Keita and ruled for one year. Mansa Maghan engaged in battles with a neighboring West African tribe called the Yatenga.

Mansa Musa Keita III: AD 1404

Mansa Musa Keita III was able to expand the territory of the Mali Empire further into the region called Dioma. Mansa Musa Keita III would pass the leadership to his brother Mansa Uli II.

Mansa Uli Keita II: AD 1460

Mansa Uli Keita engaged in battles with the neighboring Fula tribe and, in addition, the Portuguese from Europe under the command of the navigator Diogo Gomes who had attempted to invade western Africa by sea to access the natural resources of the region. The Portuguese were defeated by the Mali Empire and returned to Portugal.

Mansa Mahmud Keita II: AD 1480

Mansa Mahmud was the ruler of Mali as the empire began to decline and had to engage in war with numerous foreign and domestic powers. At this time, the West African kingdom of Songhai had also begun to rise to power and took control over the salt mines of Taghaza. The empire was also engaged in ongoing battles with the Portuguese from Europe, and the African tribe named the Yatenga again attacked Mali. In addition, the Fula tribes conducted various raids against the empire.

Mansa Mahmud Keita III: AD 1496

Mansa Mahmud had the misfortune of having to rule over a declining empire. The main rival to the Mali Empire in the West African region at this time was the Songhai Empire. The leader of the Songhai Empire at this time was Askia Muhammed I, who waged war with the Mali Empire, eventually taking control of some of its territory. In addition, another African nation called the Empire of Great Fulo, which was located just northwest of Mali, was also rising to prominence and, by AD 1490, has established its first king who battled with both the empires of Mali and Songhai. At this time, the Mali Empire began to lose more and more territory to neighboring West African states. Mansa Mahmud moved his residences farther north because of the ongoing conflicts.

Mansa Mahmud Keita IV: AD 1590

Mansa Mahmud became the final ruler of the Mali Empire and ended his rule in AD 1610. After his death, his sons fought among themselves and divided up the massively reduced now-remaining kingdom, eventually dividing the kingdom into three distinct areas, namely, Hamana, Kangaba, and Joma.

West African Muslim in Prayer

CHAPTER 15

Timeline of Ancient Mali

The Great Mosque of Djenne

80,000 BC – Africans started to move out of Africa into other regions of the planet.

10,000 BC – Rock art developed across the West African region.

500 BC – West Africans begin to work with iron and engage in iron smelting.

AD 300 – The Ghana Empire is established in western Africa.

AD 770 – The kings of the Ghana Empire have full control over the trade routes of the Sahara.

AD 1050 – King Barmandana was established as a ruler in pre-imperial Mali.

AD 1235 – The Battle of Kirina and the establishment of the Mali Empire by King Sundiata Keita occurred.

AD 1235 – Mansa Abubakari Keita became the ruler of the Mali Empire.

AD 1312 – Mansa Musa became ruler of the Mali Empire

AD 1590 – Mansa Mahmud Keita IV became the final ruler of the Mali Empire and ended his rule in AD 1610.

CHAPTER 16

Conclusion

Within this book, we have discovered some of the rich and long history of western Africa and the Mali Empire. We first focused on the expansion of the Mali Empire across the entire region of western Africa to become one of the largest and most powerful nations in history. We studied some details about the founding of this great empire and the culture of the Mandinka people. We also learned about the impact of Islam on the region and the architectural styles used by this amazing nation. We have also learned of many great kings of Mali, such as Sundiata Keita, Mansa Abubakari Keita II, and Mansa Musa. We also looked at the history of the trans-Saharan trade routes and the economy of the Mali Empire. Other key groups that we learned about that were highly influential within the Mali Empire included the griots and the Wangara. The contributions that the Mali Empire has made to world civilization are simply outstanding. I hope that his book has been an enlightening look at the history of the ancient Mali Empire and encouragement for you to research even more into the amazing historical record of Africa. We look forward to meeting with you again in future publications as we journey further into the incredible and fascinating historical records of Africa. For more information please go to www.africanempires.net

An entrance door into a mud mosque in a village in Mali